Birch*Split*Bark

Birch *Split* Bark

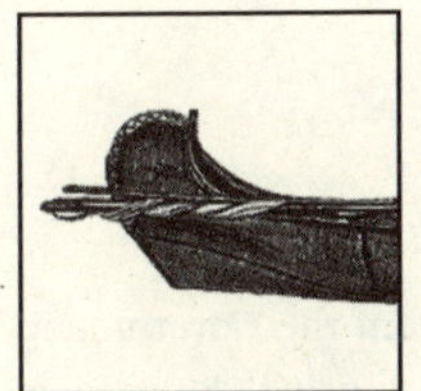
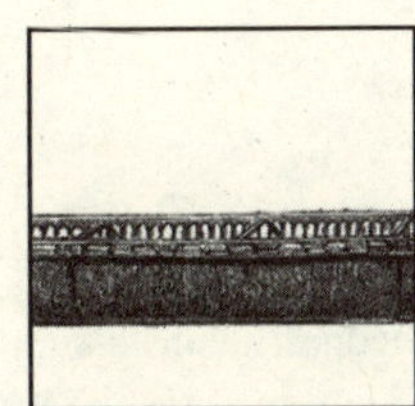
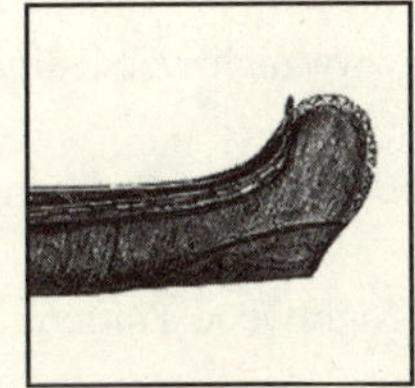

DIANE GUICHON · POEMS

Nightwood Editions · *Gibsons Landing, BC*

2007

Nightwood Editions
773 Cascade Crescent
Gibsons, BC, Canada V0N 1V9
www.nightwoodeditions.com

Designed by Carleton Wilson

Nightwood Editions acknowledges financial support from the Government of Canada through the Canada Council for the Arts and the Book Publishing Industry Development Program (BPIDP), and from the Province of British Columbia through the British Columbia Arts Council, for its publishing activities.

Printed in Canada

LIBRARY AND ARCHIVES CANADA CATALOGUING IN PUBLICATION

Guichon, Diane, 1955–
Birch split bark / Diane Guichon.

Poems.
ISBN 978-0-88971-215-7

I. Title.
PS8613.U49B57 2007 C811'.6 C2007-903922-7

for Mildred and Charles Amyot

for Dave

TABLE *of* CONTENTS

canoe
construct of bark reality
intersects white page space
letter slippage from line leader
anagram for   of possibilities
ocean

John

John's Myth – Orkneys West

Albans from France punctuate island migration
Stretch walrus skins over framework of Arctic birch branches
Hot pitch seal tar evaporated mammal oil to waterproof weatherproof
Fifty-foot curragh canoes
The smell rank of blubber diced and heated
Gristle-strained gum smoothed over gut-sewn seams
Carry valuta men through oceans of grey water white
Ice to rock beaches where tusked-tooth rich blubber tourists
Lounge in polynyas mating with others of their kind
Gannets, whales, dolphins, porpoises
Endless skeins of ducks
Ring grey harbour seals
Humpback, fin, sei
Halibut and cod
From Brittany to Orkney to Faroe to Iceland to Greenland to
Baffin Island to Labrador to New Found Land
I track sea animals and erect stone cairn markers to
Map the way
On the kill and trade
Ivory for a metallic age
To avoid Viking hordes at sea in knorrs and oar paddles gone berserking
Canoes overturned on rock walls to eke out December winds and ice-
Locked harbour doors
Tusker colonies erased from maps
Legends of Albans-in-the-West
Whisper for DNA test
To prove there: here and here
Writes home.

On a quiet, calm night in the lake country, I slink away in my canoe:

The sky swamps the water on a calm night
My address a kerosene filament that hisses in the wind
Paddle dip shatters the Milky Way
My spaceship fuelled by fifty-foot Hershey bars
To avoid Viking hordes

May 30, 1992 uppercase I appointed President . . . local chapter of canoe enthusiasts . . . with margin of . . . red wine lyrics stain
Broadsheet tablecloths
Linguistic sediments
Centrepiece remains

Beaver Club
Bastion of
Le pays d'en haut
Legacy of epicurean
Debauchery
Fillet of cod
Sauce tartare
Pork and pemmican
Boast of
Roast venison
And trade
Beaver tales

Bark sloughs away. . .

Leaf veins in my legs popping
Skin stretched over a blue couch
I flirt at the edge of water

Bark sloughs away from a scalp
Portrait of the canoe as a young man
Head stone-washed and denim wrapped

I stripped bark for a living
Poured hot pitch into boardroom meetings, then
Escaped to Baffin Island

Brides drown in tears
Children born with cauls
The canoe brought to ground

With an eye to native guides
David Thompson maps my terrain
(a pantoum repeats on the page)
I play explorer splash in the bathtub:

the main stream bends from the north on a westerly course
I assembled a string of forts unravelling from Hudson's Bay to River
Ghost
profit flows from the brigade of boats
mountain marmots whistle shrill warnings

a string of forts assembled – Hudson's Bay to Ghost River unravelling
wooden pickets driven into the ground close together a depot for
stripped pelt furs
mountain marmots whistle shrill warnings
smallpox a byword between teepees

profit flows from the brigade of boats
the main stream bends from the north on a westerly course

Fifth Avenue and Fourth Street, Calgary – January

suicide season
snow dusts granite pines planted in asphalt
grids silent symmetry of office towers
rubber trees struggle in pots under fluorescent suns
while construction crews screw windows shut

rock shafts loom through storey after storey
birds in grey pantsuits soar from floors three through thirty-six
cafeteria conversations repeat through the seasons
processed cheese melts while lettuce weeps under the weight of
forced air furnaces

he flips the pages of *Canoe and Kayak*
embossed pictures of clear June water
Kevlar and nylon hulls endure winter exposure
while he waits to wipe his ass

while the lake freezes
while the loon southern cruises
while the canoe hibernates in storage
he totals the weight of years spent in
paper labour

I adopted the native ways of weatherproofing. . .

hackmatack canoe construction
red oak keel
rabbeted to garboard plank
hackmatack root stem
trace grain curve
sometimes bend to steam

plank strake laps
crooked knife and sheaf
cedar batten bent
through ribs
support hull
tree resin pimite
seam sealer

valuta seeker
when he captured her red dress
nude doe skin condom

When my hair was long and I listened to Led Zeppelin on the radio:

I marched in a canoe protest
Against a speed race to the moon
Motors were either hidden beneath the gunwales or
Propped against the stern – at any rate we were disguised as laughter
Frayed shorts and blonde girls in pink string suits

I wore leather thongs between my toes
Slashed my jeans from bow to stern
I thought I was from Nanaimo

The canoe protest a knee-jerk monopoly
money in my pocket

I slow on my bicycle to watch hawk circles and fish rings
Slip past the lineup of half-ton trucks with motorboat
Trailers slink past the placard words
Save the Harbour Seals

My own father thirty-five years a manager for Bank of Montreal
A vested follow suit interest . . . a tradition
(a villanelle repeats on the page)

a vested interest in preserving my domain over terrain
fellows of Societies, Royal Geographical
we established camp in the pine kitchen

poured grouse out of a cereal box
heavy soak mist wets ammunition and tobacco
a vested interest in preserving their domain over terrain

map is not to scale
prepare for penetration of the mountain barrier
we established camp in the pine kitchen

mountain goats with white rumps short black horns
climb shale cliffs that guard the stream
a vested interest in preserving their domain over terrain

Blackfoot delicacies
nose entrails boiled blood and roast kidneys
we established camp in the pine kitchen

ice falls from truncated vertical strata
financed by the Western Canada Lottery, Alberta Division
a vested interest in preserving my domain over terrain
we established camp in the pine kitchen

What I packed to work each day in my briefcase:

hard sugar biscuits
pine pitch
salt pork and rum
bailing sponge   twelve voyageurs
narrow paddles   guns
an axe and sixty yards of rope
an oilskin blanket
iron cook pot
bourgeois navy beans and
mast

Keel Cruisin'

Keel cruisin'
    lane changin'
        light stop red

Left long line
    birchbark trunks
        water chute wait:
Navigators
Explorers
Pathfinders

Wheel rotations treadin' river rapids
Leavin' gas fumes in their fuckin' wake.

I join the flow of money headin' west
Retire with futures secure in my vest.

noonday sun and shore repast

canoe safari
pemmican mustard sandwich
my wife smears the map

map the safari
my wife, mustard pemmican
the canoe sandwich

The beached canoe. . .
(oral bar stool story repeats)

did you hear about the time
Lily making hot pitch

lips glued to the sap of that Enderby boy
bottom board supple root bathed in
moonshine soak my joke
their gunwales lashed together
the fuss when I discovered

did you hear
    separate strands of spruce root
    plot stones and hard lumps
    canoe mould in a building bed

no joke
to find Lily's lips glued to the boy
in the beached canoe
did you hear
    the time Kokanee canned sweat
    rang the refrain

When Mother launched Bobby from her harbour. . .

I erected a stone cairn marker in his name
And waited eighteen years to put to sea
With him bow paddling
A pair of gristle-stained men on a map track
For beer and hot wings

Skeins of ducks and other humpbacks
Buy Kokanee for their sons gone berserking

Bobby's canoe overturned while mating
Organs and instruments of locomotion arrested
The rank smell of blubber
Tuskers erased from the map

I lament the loss of walrus in pub crawls

Storm Pry

Storm pry on the inside spin
Back ferries   eddies

The wife contradicts your weather forecast
Undermines the incoming cloud formations
Tells the children, "Don't pay attention to him – he's only a halibut."

Seek your pillow or
Soft water away from the rocks
The canoe conspires against you
Fight the stream, float...

Adrift All My Life

alone on a lake
    all my life
a drift
no shore in sight
the memory of leaving land
sunk beneath storage boxes
paper lists and stalks of green tape
this house built from branches
slips from lily pad into dark water
tomorrow obscured by float debris

Isabelle

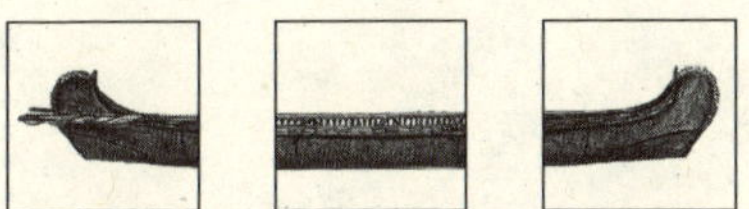

Isabelle's Myth – Ghana

Moonlight escape from Notse in Togo to
Thatched huts erected on seamless stretch of white sand beaches
Land of interlocking lagoons echo frog calls to rainbow birds in trees
Denu a name for place where palm trees kiss blue sky
Coconut retreat from white men slave traders
Dutch blunderbusses locked in waist bands
Portuguese hands grip whips
On the kill and trade
Shallow waters of the Keta keep out sailing ships
People of the Anlo Ewe foster fish nurseries
Canoe construction and shuttle between shore stations
Burned out dug out felled trees
Float a culture over sandbars and breakers
Even women and children stand upright in muddy waters
Cool their feet while the catch of the day
Herring or shark in beach-seine nets
When the lagoon dries
Salt-crusted gills sing of multiple gods and wanderlust
Groves of mango, oil-palm and fig
A stable canoe – the lemu, with a prow extension holds a steady
Course through rough surf
Between shallow inland lakes winds come and go
Narrow ripples lap front doormats
Dance drumming beats African paddling.

Doe Song

Canoe a private craft
songs lash ruddy nerves
to hearts camp lit
blade and rifle on a bed of pine boughs
leather thongs hang
in bittersweet breezes

Night tent walls
reflect crimson fire
shoulder to flank
we laughed against
granite boulders
floated smoky whispers
tales of conquest and
private water lap dances

Canoe: a paper poem romance

Birchbark paper lashed together, glued and varnished, writes a canoe upon water.

Great-grandma Rose tore off strips, pencilled poems with her back fixed against hand-crocheted cushions in cross-stitch, gazed at Great-grandpa in the stern, kneeling towards her, paddling and singing "O, come with me in my light canoe..." By their sixtieth wedding anniversary, when they gummed solid food, she'd stripped the canoe bare, only the hull remained, and a tome of nineteenth-century rhymed light verse on saturated paper.

Dip, Dip...
Carry me...
Carry me...
Lilies float...

sun disc black jet ring
smooth white sand beach walker vows
the night he proposed

I remember we stayed in bed all of one sunny Sunday at the lake. . .

sunlight on water bedroom strobe light
ceiling screen for dances
black and white flicker frames shift

eyelash flutter fans soft patter
sheets twist to silent beat
blue veins mesh at the wrist

soft slipper shuffle
cue cards oscillate under a halogen propeller
curtain cast billow
window sheers float canoe glimmer

a pulled fetus
empty cradles in her mind
lake reflects baby guilt

sun-hardened codfish
sustains the long voyage home
a highway camper convoy

bear fat daily diet
heart risk his wild adventure
loon songs block blood flow

lily bed languor
maps J stroke G spot legend
satin sheets ferment

Canoe Bingo

Cigarette smoke rises to fan
    Warn of half a house
    Around the free – space
One line anyway
Her paddle dobber in pansy colours
    Blackens undereye circles
    Wipes out numbers of other women
I from 16 to 30
    On nights he works late

behind boathouse doors
nights stroking cedar gunwales
he absents himself

I stitch and lace skins
smear bear fat to stopper holes
play supporting role

War weary, I get tired of making lunches. . .

Peanut butter and honey sandwiches
Wrapped against ant invasion

Apples mined for cores
Skins stripped leave naked white flesh

Hardened straws drill pineapple juice boxes
Raisins clump together
Safety in numbers

I thrust a tumpline across Lily's forehead
For a makeshift yoke
take weight off a weak back
her pack with binders and books
lunch her favourite manoeuvre
a solo carry over nine times eight boulders

Cocktail Party Canoeing

dip chip and glide
watercress Triscuit bite

head cheese less wild capers
drama queens wring hands gesticulate
flip hair and slide
an abyss of tweed paddles
drip wine crab
chicken livers
sniff Beaujolais lilies
spread Velveeta platter
boredom swims alongside

shrimp in frozen fetal positions
Bloody Mary sauce on the side
dip and imbibe

feet glide
hit banana dip ripple
clip linoleum pebble
eyebrows pivot
compass fallen figure
wife overboard
schmooze cruise flounders

pretensions swallow
Big Rock Honey Brown

Size eight Levi's

I slide into water at lake's edge
when the rock holding
me in place
stands up and leaves the room

water swells my cedar strips
love handles spill over the sides
of size eight Levi's

I wrinkle laying on sand
skin crackle ready for fire
survey lines crisscross a forehead
puzzled by age

the dermatologist in town barkers
too many iced creams from a corner stand
for sun spot removal
maintain a water regime

Red Cent Cedar

go by canoe
where his kisses
remember
legendary sex
shade boughs overhead

his red cent cedar paddle
an uncircumcised cock
uprooted lily bed a
lemonade stand canopy

drift on wave emotion
do not interrupt trade
blueberries smeared against canvas
stretched over ribs

deerskin or plastic basket
landward languor no protest
listen for the west wind
do not let the paddles rest

Unravelling vowels

water whispers to me in an ancient
language of vowels – *oo*'s and *aa*'s
as it wears down rocks turns them to pebbles
until he no longer gets his way
molecules separate and slip into harsh consonants
around the kitchen table – *don't*s and *didn't you*s
he packs up today's *Herald*
stashes it in his briefcase
climbs into the adored canoe and before shoving
off from the sidewalk calls over his shoulder
(a glance would have been nice)
I won't be home for dinner.
paddles like the rest of them towards the downstream
trading post where he can trade stories of beaver pelts trapped and
the wife at home.

frog calls to rainbow birds
he wants me – fetch his hammer
my feet lagoon cool

sail latitude lines
searching eider bird nest eggs
empty down filled beds

John counts it my fault
that Bobby has sex with men. I coddled or cuddled him when I should have done something else but he can't tell me what though he has some suggestions. Bobby should have worn boxers not briefs, khaki not denim, a brush cut no mushroom cap, and no cologne from the Hudson's Bay counter. He should have gone to camp on a bus with stern men, worn steel-toed boots or a brown uniform, eaten steak without a fork – no linguine with a dash of pimento, joined a team that runs a field and bashes men in padded tights, drank rye whiskey no mix from the bottle and remember, if you have to, puke behind the bleachers.

John looks outward for answers but there are no answers. Afraid of a DNA whisper he looks in the water and doesn't like the look of a homophobic, a man who looks over his shoulder at a back slap from a buddy afraid it might drift south on the current to a buttock or two.

Only thing to do is to shut up and paddle.

Bobby

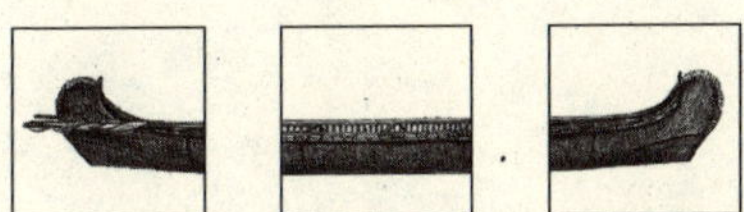

Bobby's Myth – Polynesia

creation canoe story
if you don't like your address or family debacle
go fish up a new world
Maui wears a hat for eight heads
filled with cerebral tricks
dressed in seaweed and jellyfish armor
he grabs a koi-pohaku
cuts down a koa tree

tupua tupua
carves a canoe with tattoos in bow and stern
puhi-kai ariki
paddles an outrigger with brothers past reefs and dangerous waters
sinks a magical coconut fish hook line that catches
Mr. One Tooth asleep at the bottom of the ocean
paddle paddle dear brothers

hauls in the catch of the day
rock islands and volcanoes
float a culture over sandbars and breakers

sea urchins migrate on the backs of turtles
carry valuta men through oceans of grey white water

I, the canvas sandwiched...

I, the canvas sandwiched between interior birch sheets glued into my diary every night, the subversive act of writing the only thing that keeps me from Bow River train bridge jumping in grade ten when Dad stops calling me his little buddy.

The external cedar strips my classmates see what they want to see. Conforming to chestnut model blueprints not for me.

Names they call me: *wussy boy, girly boy, homo, faggot.* I grease my skin and poke my ears with bear fat to seal tears in my fabric.

Retreat to brain tissue paper waterways unexplored by coureurs de bois, (men who by the way slept pea soup spoon fashion, ate from the same stick of pemmican, and shared paddles and pipes – their actions were never questioned!), retreat into thick hemlock forests impenetrable by cellphone ring tones.

My father's canoe mistress

my father paddled his sleek
in a red dress
banked at the River Café
beached under a patio umbrella
stroked and planed her sides
$8.99 infusion martinis
mushroom appetites

birchbark sheets no doubt
stretched over IKEA frame
four poster girl
no ballast on her
straight keel line

catapult fall
roll and never recover
my respect lost
picked up by carrion birds
on a woody trail

he preferred open water to
home interiors
divergent waves to
tap water
drains
within pipes
contained
mother no plumber

Spruce Gum Sap

chew-chew-spruce-
gum-to-soft-smack
across-my-cheek
apply-to-gap
continental di-vide
a sign-post on the Trans-
Canada High-way
Dad would not let me gear-shift
at Three Valley Gap
a pre-Sicamous sign-post
I got out at the fake western town

Nestable Canoes

nestable canoes
for shipment to rock islands and volcanoes
    where freight a consideration
designed for no tumble home
cheap rented rooms
    nest one
        within another
for ease of handling

Molecule Migration

Elongated days on the lake
Sundial baked on either side

Finger trails in water
Jeff's milk bones push us from shore

A floating dock unsecured underwater
We dabble, paddle away from the otters

No thoughts of next summer

Amphibious Shoes

(we crawled onto land)
tipped our canoe

circumnavigated
past reefs and dangerous waters
                    a backyard pool

(throw in the odd corrective stroke)
and a water-resistant rubber

amphibious shoes
ensures no blisters
when we come from water

The Price Is Right

He sits on canoe thwarts
In the living room
Docked abreast the maple coffee table
Heart strokes in rhythm to
Reruns of *The Price Is Right*
Balance sheets in his blood
Debit starboard; credit port
A father who counts fingers and toes
Liability begins in the birthing room

Paddle Slap Back

His words
Slap back
    flat stroke
        deep and back

Bile words
    cut heartwood
        stone fall to keel

Thwart words
    pitch boil
        drown out
            bailer bowl

Oar lock to ignore

Bow Legs Are Not Straight

internal tibia torsion ripped red vinyl seat
intoeing HoponPop
bow legs dr.books
knock-knees burly-bunny
greenstick fracture taupe cloth bandage

(bone healing
fibreglass cast:
birch crutch)

The Companies

alaskan campers top up bb bending branches
            bic sport bell canoe works bite footwear brooks
cascade by sport helmets chata outdoor gear columbia sportwear
     cayuga dagger drop skeg
                                                          donalco seaskinz deep see inc
easy rider rowing shells enlightened extra kayaks
sport five ten girls 4 sports folbot skins and bones glacier glove ful usa
     inc harbinger
harmony head trip helmets helly hansen hi-tech immersion research
     keen
                         jersey paddler pygmy boats kokatat watersports wear
                         ll bean
level six liquid logic lotus designs mirage truck rack merrel footwear
     montbell mountain surf
                                             inc mti murrays wind and water mysterioso
mountain man merrimack canoes outdoor supply navarro weather
     gear north water rescue company
                                                                     and paddling equipment
nrs necky kayaks os. systems palm peak uk kayaking company limited
     predator pro-tec helmets
peedee paddle paddle boy pro-tec helmets roleez wheels
rain and snow inc
stohlquist thule sweden venture kayaks
walden wildwasser sport
yakima yakpads
zoar outdoor

my life a portage

my life a portage
behind mind's curtain fall
impedes paddling to western sea
along nerve pathways
places and people
windbound cargo
I carry over boulders
yoked
across my shoulders
the canoe
I can never put down

Picture This

July twilight
Mara lake background
ash cast sunset rays
through interior smoke haze
ochre blush
fly emulsion over slate
lake extends forward to
granular depth of field

father canoe foreground
paddle at easel
fillip swing of rod
sparks angler lessons
before dark
closes mother's shutters

Pond Paddle

lake ice surface
fish rings painted red and blue
permanent markings of life beneath
surface scrape scratch rhythm of steel
sharpened keel edge to my black boot
metallic Zamboni mist
fumes rise to clouds
bent handle paddle tapered
lake surface slap

rock skips into fish net framed and
shovelled at either snow bank

Dad yells at me
words suspended in frigid air
"get'im Bob, hit'im Bob, knock'im off the puck"

my canoe tips leeward
I dip, tumble, skid
slide across the ice fall
the other team, the Crowchild Chiefs, score and
(contrary to our history) we face-off again

ice crystal comments circle our helmets
wagons drive us away

A Canoe Cult

Have you noticed the cult?
my father worships
wilderness altar incense smell of lodgepole pine needles
under sun blessings filtered through tree canopies

Have you noticed the cult?
He worships scalloped oval canoe lines
a yawning vagina chasm
that each summer travels
up the Seymour Arm to
establish a cult and tent
town in the woods fifty feet from the beach.

Notice religious leaders
with grey grizzled beards and Nehru white collars
sanctify sex with underage females or boys
in short pants who sing in a choir

Now,
vaginas do nothing for me. Poets
exalting the feminine form of breasts
and smooth apple thighs do not move me
to bar stools beside them.

Now,
kayaks offer a closed form
hole for one person to inhabit with double-edged
double paddle – the same at both ends ensure
artistic merit until logging removes larch leaf coverings
there's room in BC forests for more religious fervour
cults offering personal flotation devices
organic plankton lotion for unrestricted movement

To Bobby's father,

This letter is to explain how (very satisfied) I am with my canoe, the nestable model Chestnut of 1986. (Don't be afraid) I was afraid it would prove unsteady in open waters but it is not. (We won't ask you to attend our civil) It is roomy and very light for its size. It has resulted in increasing my already very great pleasure in canoeing (wedding ceremony). When I mount it with a lateen sail on a Canadian lake it is the real thing. The best I have ever experienced. (Perhaps in time)

Yours sincerely,
(your son-in-law to be)

J____________________

push pull slip from home. . .

a thumb thrust west
rides on the backs of loggerhead turtles
three days of black coffee and bush pissing
a change of address

    a call to Lily from Merritt
    Mr. One Tooth asleep at the bottom of the ocean

            a job unloading Montreal canoes
            prong lifts, clamps, push-pull slip sheets
            handle brand-name clothes in containers from China
            the odd dead mouse
            pulp and paper products
            bagged goods, cartons and boxes

stevedores slap my back, say
"Buddy-up to the bar, boy."
                        I buy a pair of steel-toed boots
                        and a yellow hard hat
                        to escape future damage
                        record inbound port tonnage
                        negotiate long-term rates for lay berth
                        T-shaped docking with dolphins

            I live at the point of interchange between land and water
                                                    Terminal at Port Vancouver

Lily

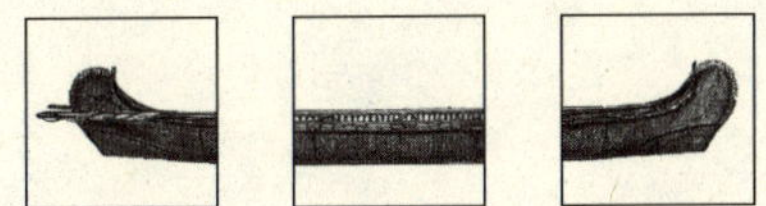

Lily's Myth – Canada

Lelawala, Oniahgahrah daughter,
creation canoe story white virtue displayed on a taupe deerskin sleeve sacrificed to tourist town maps in rotating wire sales racks a doll in white fringe dress black braids red lips oral story cataract crest brink water head rush to publish myth precipice plunge to appease purple prose tribe shaman never lets up bridal bed a rock quilt covers Canadian Shield groom waters shoved up her nose for the sake of mature harvest husks – grown yellow corn a girl a year stars in scary movie sequels of mist shrouds Three Sister Islands map the way one father cries into cold beer at the loss of a favourite daughter who mashed his corn poured his favourite hops into a leather flask of a night when snows shut wigwam doors against the water dark mark followed her crumb trail to the last page the fly leaf his death too even women and children stand upright in muddy waters.

Mara Lake

Mara Lake at the south end of a Salmon Arm and a Seymour Arm connecting to . . . should have been a hand with digits reaching up creeks to mountain peaks but instead a bowl filled with sunrise blush apples that flow down the Shuswap River in the Enderby Valley. A bowl filled with summer years of car tire tube rides, lost pink bikini bottoms and campfire sparks from the trucks gearing down for the twists in the concrete that every other year failed to avoid rock falls that mean hired high school students in yellow and orange flak jackets wave us through as we make the right-hand turn into the BC cottage road and park with our Alberta plate facing the water.

It is hard to paddle when your canoe is loaded with pig iron. . .

Father's binoculars scan the horizon and fix on Bobby's Vancouver toaster oven.

He says: *I don't want to know whose rye bread is flipped upside down for a golden finish.*

Vision framed by circular constraints though he told us each Sunday dinner to hang up the phone on the area-code loser (revealed in a technological vision – Telus connects voice and place).

Focus preset for myopic eyes.

English Bay out of range for perpetual wave beach lashings.

Call-display hang-ups are common.

The view from river centre obscured by go forth and multiply loaves and salmon have all run out of breath.

The canoe manages to right itself after each catapult fall.

Junior High

skin marquee
birchbark knobs and warts
red patches shale rock squeezed
dot my face

pine gum
keelside press
under maple desk
slate bored

hormones shank a hook
gossip stopper knot
stanchion friend
anchors tag end
prevents fray

I lash lanyard to
tow-line leader

Father Chasm

One summer I attempted to build a canoe bridge over the father chasm to seek rainbow pot of approval, gold if you can get it. Mapped a watercourse for tandem paddling but curse it if loony moon cycles did not put me on an inside spin facing strong westerly wind. Father took up power strokes in bow position calling out directions as usual this time on how I should J stern stroke. When he wasn't looking over his shoulder I let him down, my paddle tired and out of work on my knee. Father carried me to the portage point where I stepped off the dock and secured moorage to a law library fallen logbook of case studies. The last sight I had of him that summer – his back ebbing away from me.

Nail Beauty
(a villanelle repeats polish)

i cruise the aisle at Shoppers Drug Mart
search for wet look nail colour – l'orèal steel
a hand job to smooth varnish over cedar planks

Dad said to remove moss cuticle from canoe rivets
tired of Sunday work in the boathouse
i cruise the aisle at Shoppers Drug Mart

the girls wanna meet Tom in the park at 3:00
he's been hanging around my locker leering
a hand job to smooth varnish over cedar planks

i hear by way of Nicki then Karen that Tom's coming
confidence sinks under date pressure
i cruise the aisle at Shoppers Drug Mart

if i promise to remove moss
if i string Dad a line maybe i'll get to
a hand job to smooth varnish over cedar planks

are those rivets polished yet?
zits erupt when i'm upset
i cruise the aisle at Shoppers Drug Mart
a hand job to smooth varnish over cedar planks

Mother Prefers Maple Paddles

Mother prefers maple paddles with lengths from five to six feet to stir chocolate batter, whip waves by hand instead of mix master. The scoop spoon varnished ready lies across her knees while she searches the bowl for turtles swimming under the surface, letting me lick stainless steel in the stern. Her Queen Elizabeth hat with a black crow feather stuck in the rim shades her eyes from fluorescent glare. Turn the oven off, she shouts to the skylight. I'm baking down here. She plucks pine resin from her blouse and points to the lily fronds that bounce and wait near shore – icing on the cake for my twelfth night.

My mother cooking without a recipe always an adventure in unchartered waters on a Sunday after the loon goes down.

An Umbrella

the canoe an umbrella, goosebump arms and legs
tucked under trim, protection gymnastics
rainwater barrel roll, upside down keel
the first time my brother told me
he preferred boys over girls
beach
sand
edged
our
shorts
and
crept
into
rock
crevices
to
avoid
the
deluge

Spirit Canoe

Mother drives me to church at St. Peter's in Salmon Arm where we prayed to God the Almighty Manitou. Fingertip paddles and palm fronds pressed together to sign the canoe. Jesus's twelve stations of the cross a long portage around earth's sins to unmapped waters. He dragged his cedar dug-out up the hill to Calvary over sedimentary rock. If Father had followed indoor religion he could have told Jesus that for a solo carry some people lash canoe paddles across the centre thwart as a makeshift yoke or thrust a tumpline across the carrier's forehead to take weight off a weak back.

Our communion 11 a.m. mass of bacon on the barbeque, eggs and pancakes in the pan. We bow our heads in the presence of a Pacific wind. Thank you for tree-tapped maple syrup from Chicoutimi and Invermere Kicking Horse River coffee. After brunch Bobby and I skip to the beach and draw canoe symbols in the sand, fish without the two-point tail. Father, son and ghost of a mother guide my spirit canoe.

The Will

Dead at seventy-four of heart failure while carrying a green garbage bag of Dr. Pepper cans and Kokanee to the recycling depot between the river and the Okanagan Highway. A man not large as he lies in his canoe in Enderby but even dead he emits odours. Throw 50 percent of my ashes into the Shuswap River from the Enderby Bridge at 6:30 a.m. on a Tuesday in June. Sink the other 50 percent with my canoe at the base of the rope-swing cliff on Mara Lake. I'd been living in the city ten years when he died. I'd forgotten how slow the drive could be westbound on the Trans-Canada following families in covered wagons and Winnebagos and trucks in it for the long haul. The cans paid out seven dollars twenty-five cents. The woman came to his funeral wanting to know what to do with the change. He was a stickler for recycling so why sink a good canoe. Three toonies, one loonie and a red poppy quarter. No Flanders Field for this Captain Canoe. He sunk the canoe once before when he was building it in order to swell and seal the wood latte straps.

Ragweed Sunrise

grad night verdant taffeta
urethane slip out early from canoe cockpit condoms
to avoid multi-legged boatmen
bedding down

bra straps fight buoyant river
Kokanee current culprit
enter spin zone – not enough water
stomach froths face
careens downstream eddy
cargo multiple spills

solo limp trip
canoe runs aground
shore ragweed scrape
sunrise leaks between
eyelid rust wiped away
mop-headed date floats home
wrapped soaked
taffeta shroud

The Acme of Perfection

The acme of perfection has been reached in the construction of the featherweight canoe. By eliminating every ounce of weight that can possibly be done away with and by using extra light wood, carefully selected as to strength, we are able to produce a strong, sturdy canoe that will carry two men and a load, the weight with light shoe keel being only 34½ to 35 pounds. This weight is a mere nothing on a portage and this craft can easily be taken in to almost inaccessible lakes where the big fish hide and where it is quite necessary to have an easily handled craft to get them.

While he slid a fat rounded grub on my hook as bait Father told me that boys do not like girls with extra pound rolls around their thwarts.

Daddy kowtow

with every screen door bang
    cold air creeps in
Mother jumps
Brother picks up the remote
I open a book about Swiss mountain girl who tames grouchy grandfather with her blonde pigtails bib apron. (My father's father beat my father with paint stick slap to the back of father's hand twice daily mother tells me instead of reading *Heidi* at bedtime.) No excuse for bad behaviour I hear from He who casts a long sharp fish-hook line of dialogue to reel in small and moderate-sized trout.

I Need a Sponson

I need a sponson canoe to survive a day on the water with my father. A canoe with floatation chambers attached to the sides to reduce any possibility of upset.

"What are you doing working a minimum-wage job serving eggs on a plate in Field, BC, a pit-stop place setting on the side of the road?" said Father.

Why did I keep coming back to get dish wiped over and over?

"Egg yolk is hard to remove once dried on enamel," said Lily.

(Egg white sticks in the whisker stubble face of opposition.)

"Shut up and paddle."

finger point amble

father reads maps east to west, strikes a direct route, time and distance factors in math equations that saw hudson's bay and canadian pacific buy land beside and beneath railroad tracks and rivers.

i enter at a point where my finger points and amble. my nose might face forward but my ponytail sticks out backwards or the ring circles my finger before i fling bread crumbs eaten by seagulls as they kiss the water. points matter less than where the i finds itself when you have to go to the bathroom.

Fibreglass Dabble

She dabbled in her fibreglass canoe around the bay of crystal sands.

He jetted downriver from Enderby. Pulled alongside in his silver and red seadoo.

He threatened to swamp her where he stood upon the water.

His hands played with the handlebars. Water ribbons dripped from their endless meetings.

> *Throw me a rope and I'll drag you behind.*
> *No thanks. You'd sink me.*

Aviator glasses, spiked blonde hair.

He spun a few tight wheelies that sent her rockin'.

He left a trail of oil behind on the water. Rainbow promise in the slick but the sun disappeared behind a hover cloud.

She met him in town at the ice cream shoppe in the narrows.

> *So you shook off the old relic.*
> *No, it's parked at the dock. I don't require speed,* she said in the haughty canoe voice of a Green Party member.

Summer nights that stretch all the way to English Bay.

Night flies track around dock lamps.

Growth hormones navigate arteries built for laughter. Shakespearean lake dance of nymphs where no one can see their tentacle embrace – poetry in action.

Long bones, hairless chest tanned peach pit taupe, a cockiness between his shoulder blades that doesn't disappear even when her father catches them beneath her fibreglass beach blanket after moonrise.

Mature harvest husk and grown yellow corn.

Oniagahrah daughter.

Ashes lined the shore. . .

We laid him to rest in his coffin in his best rainmaker suit with his arms crossed above his sword and his beloved Canadian Shield. We rolled him down the beach on fallen timber logs and shoved him into the furnace. Mother, soaked in alcohol, set the casket aflame. The funeral pyre burned all night and into the middle of the lake. Ashes lined the shore in the morning.

We drove into Enderby in his blue 1990 Ford Explorer to pick out an urn. For Mother a red cedar box that matched her vanity scarf. For Bobby and me – the Grecian urn, perpetual centaurs, half-men, half-horse, chasing half-naked girls around and around the bowl's base into the next century.

The funeral director poured Father into the urn spilling an arm or a leg onto the indoor-outdoor faux Persian carpet. We carried Father out to the car in a brown paper bag. Father's spirit sat strapped into the backseat beside a Safeway bag of Longview beef jerky and Bobby's twenty-four pack of Pale Ale. Mother cried. She dabbed at her eyes with a green tartan hanky so mascara would not run away down her cheeks and onto the next Greyhound bus to Vancouver.

My father's lap

on a green Scots print cushion rocking in the corner cage
the smell of pine in a lumberjack red and black checked shirt pocket
corduroy grey feathers dried red paint plaid
in from the boathouse where he roosts in summer
I climb the branches of the chair and rest against his truncated speech
his song catches my ear

Rope jumps and pansies. . .

I push off from the beach at the Hummingbird Hotel and climb into the stern.

I'd tucked Dad in the night before, stowing his urn tight under the forward thwart. His urn half full half empty depending on your life philosophy. (I'd already tossed 50 percent of his life away over the fishing bridge in Enderby. Maybe 45 or 55 percent. Sorry Dad, hard to quantify life's ashes.)

Sun from the east lights the rock cliff before me. The lake a green malt beer without the lively foam.

No speedboats in sight. I paddle.

The swing rope hooked on its lodgepole pine overhang.

I float just off the rocks that sunk my stomach as a child.

Jump Lily. Swing out. Jump.

A good twenty feet to water. One woman's blood marks the spot where she failed to let go the week before.

We're not leaving until you jump.

My feet sore from the barefoot climb. Dad in the boat below. Another dad plays executioner and passes me the rope. Kids line up behind me impatient for their own dive drop. Get on with it, would ya.

Water soft up close forms concrete crust at a distance.

I rock the boat until the gunwales touch water.

I jump.

Lake water streams into my nose.

I lean on the canoe's lip. Water fills its bottom. I slip further into the chill. Father slips out too. His urn hovers a foot beneath the surface and then sinks into glacial remains.

The canoe floats beside me just under the edge of water. It refuses to sink.

A fisherman in an aluminum dory with outboard motor helps me rescue the canoe from last breath language. We make our way to shore.

The canoe suntans on my ninth-floor balcony in Calgary. Home to pansies petunias and green prairie grasses.

I poke holes in its bottom so the water can run away. So the flowers won't drown.

Not My River

his river not my river
a flash of fin or bobber twitch and a salmon leap
not in my memory of rubber tires and blow holes
the plastic plug digging into my inner tube thigh
leg dangle stream ride
Angela's giggles when we upturned
spilled our sunshine oil all over petrified river rock where
by custom he stood to cast his line to the far shore
horizon eyes ignore the life
rafts pass him by
the river flows into Mara Lake, as always

like white birch

like white birch I am not what I am on the exterior. White on the squirrel track trunk but stripped and turned red bark dark interior reveals a different me. Stretched over cedar planks me re-imagines the limits of skin and lowercase i's float on green or blue, blend with shore brown. Exterior skin cups the multiple, reveals the prism colours of who we keep to ourselves.

Acknowledgements

Special thanks to my children, Nicki, Davey and Tyler, who encouraged and praised my efforts at university while reminding me that my interest in Canadian canoe poems and canoe representations in Canadian culture confirmed my status as "geek."

I would like to thank my husband, Dave, for his constant love, support and encouragement to freely pursue poetry, an activity that has brought me immeasurable pleasure.

Notes

The poem "Doe Song" (p. 34) is written as a tribute to Isabella Valancy Crawford (1850–1887) and her canoe poem "Said the Canoe."

The poem "Red Cent Cedar" (p. 48) blends language from three other canoe poems by female Canadian poets: Isabella Valancy Crawford's "The Lily Bed," E. Pauline Johnson's "The Idlers," and Anneharte Baker's "Blueberry Canoe" (from *Baker's Exercises in Lip Pointing*. Vancouver: North Star. 2003).

The poem "To Bobby's father" (p. 71) contains found language from letters written to the Chestnut Canoe Company. (Solway, Kenneth. *The Story of the Chestnut Canoe: 150 Years of Canadian Canoe Building*. Halifax: Nimbus, 1997).

About the Author

Diane Guichon is a recent MA graduate in creative writing from the University of Calgary. Her poetry sequence *Vignettes* was adapted for the stage and performed by the Nickle and Dime Production Company in 2006. She currently lives with her family in Calgary, where she teaches writing. *Birch Split Bark* is her first book.